Presented to

_____

by_____

on_____

Who Made the World?

Kathleen Long Bostrom
Illustrated by Elena Kucharik

Tyndale House Publishers, Inc.
CAROL STREAM, ILLINOIS

Visit Tyndale's exciting Web site for kids at www.tyndale.com/kids

TYNDALE is a registered trademark of Tyndale House Publishers, Inc.
Tyndale Kids logo is a trademark of Tyndale House Publishers, Inc.

Little Blessings is a registered trademark of Tyndale House Publishers, Inc.
The Little Blessings characters are a trademark of Elena Kucharik.

Who Made the World?

Designed by Jacqueline L. Nuñez
Edited by Stephanie Voiland

Scripture quotations are taken from the *Holy Bible*, New Living Translation, copyright © 1996, 2004, 2007
by Tyndale House Foundation. Used by permission of Tyndale House Publishers, Inc., Carol Stream, Illinois
60188. All rights reserved.

Library of Congress Cataloging-in-Publication Data

Bostrom, Kathleen Long.
  Who made the world? / Kathleen Long Bostrom ; illustrated by Elena Kucharik.
      p. cm.
  "Tyndale kids."
  ISBN 978-1-4143-2011-3 (hc)
  1. Creation--Juvenile literature. I. Kucharik, Elena. II. Title.
  BT695.B59 2009
  231.7'65--dc22
                                    2008051592

Printed in Singapore

15 14 13 12 11 10 09
7 6 5 4 3 2 1

To my beloved uncle David:
From the beginning, you have been a special part of my life,
and you always will be. Love to you and dear Paige,
—K. B.

To Emelia, our newest Little Blessing.
Love always,
—E. K.

The world is so pretty!

There's so much to see.

A rainbow! A river!

A flower! A tree!

So who made the world?

God, I *think* it was you.

Did you have a helper?

If so, tell me who!

What was the first thing
you made, and the last?
Did you snap your fingers
to make it go fast?

You must have been busy—

how long did it take?

At night, did you sleep?

Did you stay wide awake?

What was the hardest,

and what was most fun?

The plants or the stars

or the people—which one?

If you had it all
　to do over again,
would you make the world
　as you did way back then?

How can I ever

say thank you enough

for making a world

with such wonderful stuff?

One final question

I'm puzzling through:

If you made it all,

well, then, God—who made you?

You've asked some great questions—

you sound very smart!

Now open your Bible.

See there, at the start,

are some of the answers

to questions you seek.

And now, turn the page—

it is God's turn to speak!

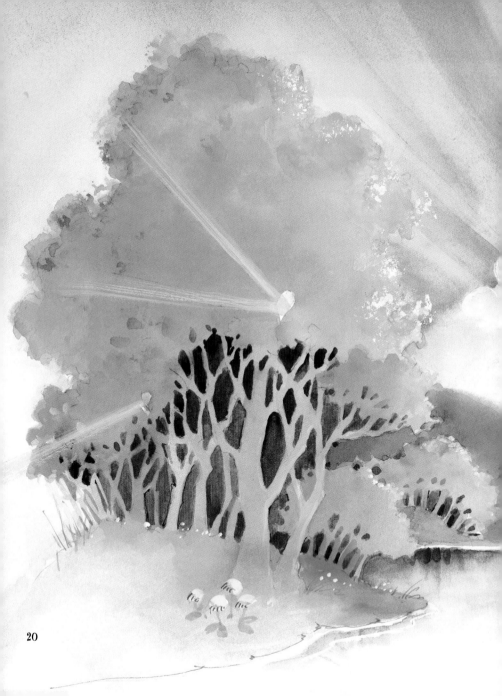

It's hard to believe

that there ever could be

a time when the only one

living was me.

22

Yet in the beginning,

  way back at the start,

the Spirit and Jesus

  were there, taking part.

23

I looked all around;

it was empty and dark.

I had an idea—

just a glimmer, a spark.

I took a deep breath

and said, "Let there be light!"

That's how it first started:

with day and with night.

On I continued

with sky and the seas,

land filled with grasses

and flowers and trees.

29

Then came the seasons,

the sun and the moon.

Fish and then birds,

with their chirp-chirping tune.

Next, I made creatures
of all different types,
from polka-dot pandas
to zebras with stripes!

The days rolled along,

    and then lickety-split—

I'm finished! *I thought,*

    but before I could quit . . .

Something was missing;

I could not be through

until I created

the people—like you!

People are special!

How so? Here's the key:

people are made

in the image of me!

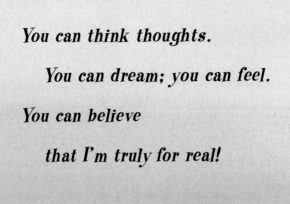

You can think thoughts.

    You can dream; you can feel.

You can believe

    that I'm truly for real!

41

How many days

did it take me? Just six!

I did not need magic

or use any tricks.

I never need sleep,

 but I did take a rest.

Yet not till I finished—

 I gave it my best!

Nothing was hard;

I enjoyed every minute.

I love the whole world!

I love everything in it!

If I could go back,

I would not change a thing.

But wait till you see

what the future will bring!

All of creation

will sparkle like new.

My home will be earth,

and I'll live there, with you!

The best way to thank me?

Here's a good way:

Sing and be happy!

Enjoy every day.

Always be kind

to the people you meet.

Don't ever litter,

and keep the world neat.

Where do I come from?

It's hard to explain.

When all's said and done,

a few questions remain.

All I can say is that
no one made me.
I've been here forever
and always will be.

Although I made

    everything living, it's true,

I cannot imagine

    the world without you!

Bible References

Here are some Bible verses to talk about as you read this book again with your child. You may want to open your Bible as you read the verses. This will help your little one understand that God's answers in this poem come from his Word, the Bible.

It's hard to believe that there ever could be
a time when the only one living was me.

> God made the earth by his power, and he preserves it by his wisdom. With his own understanding he stretched out the heavens. Jeremiah 10:12

> When he spoke, the world began! It appeared at his command. Psalm 33:9

Yet in the beginning, way back at the start,
the Spirit and Jesus were there, taking part.

> The Spirit of God was hovering over the surface of the waters. Genesis 1:2

> In the beginning the Word already existed. The Word was with God, and the Word was God. He existed in the beginning with God. God created everything through him, and nothing was created except through him. John 1:1-3

I looked all around; it was empty and dark.
I had an idea—just a glimmer, a spark.

> The earth was formless and empty, and darkness
> covered the deep waters. And the Spirit of God was
> hovering over the surface of the waters.
> Genesis 1:2

I took a deep breath and said, "Let there be light!"
That's how it first started: with day and with night.

> God said, "Let there be light," and there was light. And
> God saw that the light was good. Then he separated
> the light from the darkness. God called the light "day"
> and the darkness "night." Genesis 1:3-5

> The Lord merely spoke, and the heavens were cre-
> ated. He breathed the word, and all the stars were
> born. Psalm 33:6

On I continued with sky and the seas,
land filled with grasses and flowers and trees.

> God called the space "sky." And evening passed and
> morning came, marking the second day. Genesis 1:8

> God called the dry ground "land" and the waters
> "seas." And God saw that it was good. Then God said,
> "Let the land sprout with vegetation—every sort of
> seed-bearing plant, and trees that grow seed-bearing
> fruit." Genesis 1:10-11

Then came the seasons, the sun and the moon.
Fish and then birds, with their chirp-chirping tune.

God said, "Let lights appear in the sky to separate the day from the night. Let them be signs to mark the seasons, days, and years. Genesis 1:14

God made two great lights—the larger one to govern the day, and the smaller one to govern the night. Genesis 1:16

God said, "Let the waters swarm with fish and other life. Let the skies be filled with birds of every kind." Genesis 1:20

Next, I made creatures of all different types,
from polka-dot pandas to zebras with stripes!

God said, "Let the earth produce every sort of animal, each producing offspring of the same kind—livestock, small animals that scurry along the ground, and wild animals." Genesis 1:24

The days rolled along, and then lickety-split—
I'm finished! I thought, but before I could quit . . .
Something was missing; I could not be through
until I created the people—like you!

God said, "Let us make human beings in our image, to be like us." Genesis 1:26

People are special! How so? Here's the key:
people are made in the image of me!

> God created human beings in his own image. In the
> image of God he created them; male and female he
> created them. Genesis 1:27

> The Lord . . . makes us more and more like him as we
> are changed into his glorious image. 2 Corinthians 3:18

You can think thoughts. You can dream; you can feel.
You can believe that I'm truly for real!

> You must love the LORD your God with all your heart,
> all your soul, all your mind, and all your strength.
> Mark 12:30

> Faith is the confidence that what we hope for will
> actually happen; it gives us assurance about things we
> cannot see. Hebrews 11:1

> Blessed are those who believe without seeing me.
> John 20:29

How many days did it take me? Just six!
I did not need magic or use any tricks.

> In six days the LORD made the heavens, the earth, the
> sea, and everything in them; but on the seventh day he
> rested. Exodus 20:11

> By faith we understand that the entire universe was
> formed at God's command, that what we now see did
> not come from anything that can be seen. Hebrews 11:3

I never need sleep, but I did take a rest.
Yet not till I finished—I gave it my best!

> [The Lord] will not let you stumble; the one who watches over you will not slumber. Indeed, he who watches over Israel never slumbers or sleeps. Psalm 121:3-4

> On the seventh day God had finished his work of creation, so he rested from all his work. Genesis 2:2

Nothing was hard; I enjoyed every minute.
I love the whole world! I love everything in it!

> God looked over all he had made, and he saw that it was very good! Genesis 1:31

> You are worthy, O Lord our God, to receive glory and honor and power. For you created all things, and they exist because you created what you pleased. Revelation 4:11

If I could go back, I would not change a thing.
But wait till you see what the future will bring!

> I saw a new heaven and a new earth, for the old heaven and the old earth had disappeared. And the sea was also gone. Revelation 21:1

All of creation will sparkle like new.
My home will be earth, and I'll live there, with you!

> Look, God's home is now among his people! He will live with them, and they will be his people. God himself will be with them. Revelation 21:3

The best way to thank me? Here's a good way:
Sing and be happy! Enjoy every day.

> Sing a new song to the LORD! Let the whole earth sing
> to the LORD! Sing to the LORD; praise his name. Each
> day proclaim the good news that he saves.
> Psalm 96:1-2

Always be kind to the people you meet.
Don't ever litter, and keep the world neat.

> Be kind to each other. Ephesians 4:32

> You must not defile the land where you live, for I live
> there myself. Numbers 35:34

Where do I come from? It's hard to explain.
When all's said and done, a few questions remain.

> Now we see things imperfectly, like puzzling reflections
> in a mirror, but then we will see everything with per-
> fect clarity. All that I know now is partial and incom-
> plete, but then I will know everything completely, just
> as God now knows me completely.
> 1 Corinthians 13:12

All I can say is that no one made me.
I've been here forever and always will be.

> I am . . . the First and the Last, the Beginning and the
> End. Revelation 22:13

Christ is the visible image of the invisible God. He existed before anything was created and is supreme over all creation, for through him God created everything in the heavenly realms and on earth. He made the things we can see and the things we can't see. Colossians 1:15-16

Although I made everything living, it's true, I cannot imagine the world without you!

When I look at the night sky and see the work of your fingers—the moon and the stars you set in place—what are mere mortals that you should think about them, human beings that you should care for them? Yet you made them only a little lower than God and crowned them with glory and honor. Psalm 8:3-5

The God of Israel . . . is the Creator of everything that exists. Jeremiah 10:16

About the Author

Kathleen Bostrom has been an ordained minister in the Presbyterian Church (USA) since 1983. She and her husband, Greg, have served as copastors of Wildwood Presbyterian Church in Wildwood, Illinois, since 1991.

Kathy has won awards for preaching and is often requested to speak to groups at the national level. She has published numerous articles in various journals and newspapers, and is the author of over a dozen books for children. *Who Is Jesus?* was a finalist for the 2000 Gold Medallion Award, and *What about Heaven?* was nominated for the People's Choice Award. Kathy's books have sold well over one million copies.

Kathy has been a board member of the Presbyterian Writers Guild since 1998 and has served as president. She is also a member of the Society of Children's Book Writers and Illustrators.

Kathy earned a master of arts in Christian education and a master of divinity from Princeton Theological Seminary, and a doctor of ministry in preaching from McCormick Theological Seminary in Chicago.

Kathy and Greg have three children: Christopher, Amy, and David.

About the Illustrator

Elena Kucharik, well-known Care Bears artist, has created the Little Blessings characters that appear in the line of Little Blessings products for young children and their families.

Born in Cleveland, Ohio, Elena received a bachelor of fine arts degree in commercial art at Kent State University. After graduation she worked as a greeting card artist and art director at American Greetings Corporation in Cleveland.

For most of her career, Elena has been a freelance illustrator. She was the lead artist and developer of Care Bears, as well as a designer and illustrator for major corporations and publishers. Most recently Elena has been focusing her talents on illustrations for children's books.

Elena and her husband live in Madison, Connecticut. They have two grown daughters and three adorable grandchildren.

Books in the Little Blessings line

- *Prayers for Little Hearts*
- *Questions from Little Hearts*

- *What Is God Like?*
- *Who Is Jesus?*
- *What about Heaven?*
- *Are Angels Real?*
- *What Is Prayer?*
- *Is God Always with Me?*
- *Why Is There a Cross?*
- *What Is the Bible?*
- *Who Made the World?*

- *The One Year Devotions for Preschoolers*
- *The One Year Devotions for Preschoolers 2*
  (available soon)

- *God Loves You*
- *Thank You, God!*
- *Many-Colored Blessings*
- *Blessings Come in Shapes*

- *God Created Me!*
  A memory book of baby's first year

CP0216